Jay's Space

Jay's Space

A Story of Autism, Movement, and Acceptance

Vi Lewis

JAYpublishingDen LLC

This book is a work of creative nonfiction inspired by lived experience.

DEDICATION

For Jayden,
who is still the who that he is.

For Heather,
who calls him her friend.

And for the children
who speak through motion,
silence,
and being.

JAYDEN

Jayden is autistic. This book is a poem of the spaces he lived in as child, and still lives in. spinning, laughing, jumping, pausing, singing and simply being the who that he is.

Jayden just turned 20, because autistic children will become autistic adults. There will be new spaces, but some spaces will remain.

The book is for caregivers, children, and anyone who has ever wanted to understand without asking why.

He wakes every
morning
to the who that he
is.
He seems okay
to be who he is.
He wakes with a
smile.

And sometimes,
I hear him laughing.

I peek in his room.
His face is in the mirror.
He's making funny faces,
laughing at his laughs.

Now he's jumping,
and jumping again.
A few more jumps,
and maybe he'll stop.

He pauses when he stops,
as if to say:
I don't know why I just did that...I
need to do it again

Jump!

He spins around.
Around and around he goes.
Two or three more spins,
and then he stops.

Again, he takes a
pause,
As if asking himself:
Why did I do that?
He doesn't know why.
And neither do I.

I say, "Good morning."
He doesn't reply.
He smiles. Yes, he smiles.
And in his eyes, I hear him say
loud and clear – Good morning.

I know that's what he's saying
because he smirks,
sometimes squints,
as if asking,
Good morning, so what's for
breakfast today?

The mouse glides in his hand,
He is in his world.

hand raised unnoticed,

Hand down
tap sound
shoulders square

then relax, so quick.
the art continues
no interruption to creativity.

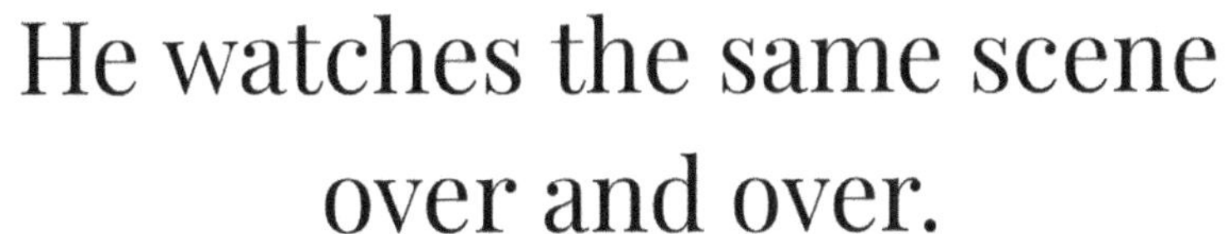

He watches the same scene
over and over.
His finger glide
back,
again,
again.
He smiles,
he laughs.

This morning he watched his cartoons
Same episode
Over and over again.
I didn't watch the episode.
But now I watch him perform
Now I listen.
And I watch.

He plays each character
repeat every word.
Every expression.
Every movement.
Delivering dialogue with precison.

If you missed his performance
Don't worry
There'll be another
Later, tomorrow or the next day
And just like today
He won't miss a beat.

open palm – Any surface
Table, wall, floor.
tap, tap, tap,
Just to be.
Just because.

open palm,
tap, tap, tap
table, wall, floor.
no pattern – no pause.

His open palm finds
whatever is closest.
not nervous,
not impatient
just there.
At that moment.
A tap
A sound.

STOMP!

Sometimes he's quiet.
Ever so quiet.
Not empty
Not lost
still full
of the who that he is.
just full
in a different way.
so quiet.
I listen
With my eyes.

a soundless sound

And sometimes,
even when I don't,
I hear the sound
through the look in his eyes.
It's a soundless sound.
Ever so quiet,
and yet so loud.

"BECAUSE AUTISTIC CHILDREN BECOME ADULT..."

Some things soften,
Some things shift,
And some remain.

A stomp sudden,
grounded.
A moment of stillness
inside the movement.
Then release.
And he continues,
as if nothing happened.

"The movements shown in this book are often referred to as stimming, self-stimulatory behaviors that help regulate sensory and emotional experiences."

Each day is a learning process
for him,
and for me.
I am learning
to give him his space.
To laugh with his laughs.
Spin with his spins.
Jump with his jumps.
Stomp with his stomps.
Tap with his taps.
Knowing tomorrow,
he'll wake
as the who that he is.
And that's okay
for me,
and for him.
For his sake,
to feel free
and to belong.
yet strong enough

to sing his song
and be who he is.

I must learn acceptance of him,
and continue embracing
the who that he is.

And if there are hidden things
yet to be discovered,
to help or guide,
I do it with care.

I listen with my eyes.
And I continue to hear
and understand
his soundless sounds.

And I continue to embrace
the who that he is
not as a baby,

not only the little boy
he was, and is,

And I continue to embrace
the who that he is
not as a baby,
not only the little boy
he was, and is,
but as the young man
he is becoming.
Different,
but the same.

AUTHOR'S NOTE

I wrote this book for my grandson, and for all the kids and young people like him who are seen through labels before they are recognized as individuals.

This book isn't about fixing, correcting, or explaining. It's about noticing them and taking the time to listen and engage with them when you can.

Jayden has shown me that giving space can be a form of love.

This book is for those who express themselves through movement, silence, creativity, and being, and for those who are learning how to listen.

ABOUT AUTISM

Many autistic children communicate through physical actions. They may spin, jump, pace, clap, or remain quiet.

These behaviors are referred to as "stimming," which is an abbreviation for self-stimulation or self-regulation.

Jayden's movements is a part of his identity. They reflect his joy, his means of expression, his curiosity, and his sense of comfort.

The book does not tell Jayden to stops, it works to understand and accept.

ABOUT BOOK

An excellent resource for educators, therapists, and caregivers that may prove beneficial when engaging with an autistic child:

- It fosters empathy and understanding.

- It addresses sensory experiences without delving into explanations, as it is based on lived experiences rather than academic studies.

- It affirms the autistic identity through shared experiences.

- It encourages discussions regarding movement, silence, and personal space.

This book does not provide an explanation of autism; rather, it serves as a testament to it.

- About 1 in 100 children globally is diagnosed with autism spectrum disorder (ASD).

- Autism has increased over the past few decades.

- Boys are diagnosed with autism at a rate four times higher than girls.

- Early diagnosis and intervention is a key to help, not cure.

- Autism affects individuals across all racial, ethnic, and economic groups.

Other Books About Autism
By Vi Lewis

Sorry If I Disturb You – Jayden A Boy With Autism

Revised Edition (2026) – Now Available

Originally published in 2014 and embraced by readers, this updated edition continues the journey with rcnewed clarity, insight, and voice.

Stay In Line With Me: A Coloring & Poetry Book For Kids With Autism

Published 2017